AN ARKFUL OF
ANIMALS

AN ARKFUL OF
ANIMALS

Selected by William Cole

Illustrated by Lynn Munsinger

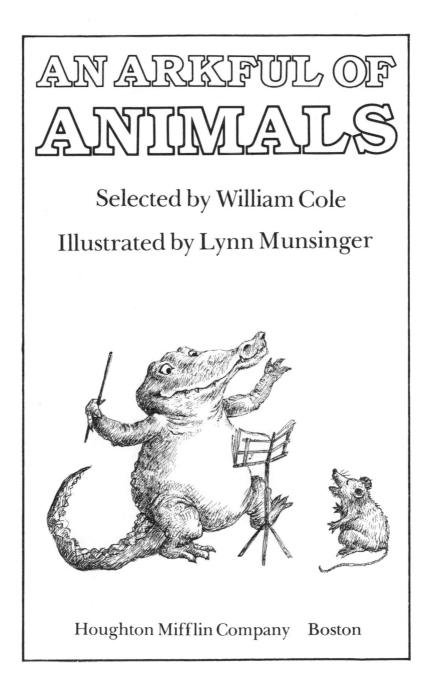

Houghton Mifflin Company   Boston

Library of Congress Cataloging in Publication Data
Main entry under title:

An Arkful of animals.

    Includes indexes.
    SUMMARY: A collection of poems by famous poets
featuring owls, oliphaunts, and other familiar and
fanciful creatures.
    1. Animals – Juvenile poetry.   [1.   Animals – Poetry.
2.   Poetry – Collections]   I.   Cole, William, 1919-
II.   Munsinger, Lynn.
PN6110.C4A73   821'.008'036   78-70041

    ISBN 0-395-27205-X   PA ISBN 0-395-61618-2

Printed in the United States of America
Copyright acknowledgments are at the back of the book.
VB   10   9   8   7

See the animals — what an arkful!
Of squirrels and pigeons, there's a parkful;
Dogs, hyenas — how it's barkful;
All that singing means it's larkful!

And outside, the seas are sharkful.

AN ARKFUL OF
ANIMALS

Old Noah's Ark

FOLK RHYME

Old Noah once he built an ark,
And patched it up with hickory bark.
He anchored it to a great big rock,
And then he began to load his stock.
The animals went in one by one,
The elephant chewing a carroway bun.
The animals went in two by two,
The crocodile and the kangaroo.
The animals went in three by three,
The tall giraffe and the tiny flea,
The animals went in four by four,
The hippopotamus stuck in the door.
The animals went in five by five,
The bees mistook the bear for a hive.
The animals went in six by six,
The monkey was up to his usual tricks.
The animals went in seven by seven,
Said the ant to the elephant, "Who're ye shov'n?"
The animals went in eight by eight,
Some were early and some were late.
The animals went in nine by nine,
They all formed fours and marched in a line.
The animals went in ten by ten,
If you want any more, you can read it again.

The Owl

CONRAD AIKEN

To whit
to whoo
he stares
right through
whatever
he looks at
maybe
YOU
and so
whatever
else
you do
don't
    ever
        ever
           be
             a
                mouse
            or
          if
        you
  are
    STAY
      IN
        YOUR
          HOUSE

old owl
can you be really
wise
and do those great big
sunflower eyes
see THINGS
that WE
can never see
perched on the tiptop of your tree
or by jiminy
on a chimney
or whooshing by
on velvet wings?
Let's hie to bed
and leave him be.

Little Miss Limberkin

MARY MAPES DODGE

Little Miss Limberkin,
Dreadful to say,
Found a mouse in the cupboard
Sleeping away.
Little Miss Limberkin
Gave such a scream,
She frightened the little mouse
Out of its dream.

The Snail

WILLIAM COLE

As everyone knows,
Wherever he goes
The snail
Leaves a trail
Of goo —
Like glue.

I don't —
Do you?

Easy Diver

ROBERT FROMAN

Pigeon on the roof.
Dives.
Go-
ing
fa-
st.

G
O
I
N
G
T
O

HIT HARD!

Opens wings.

Softly, gently,

down.

Old Grey Goose

HARRY BEHN

Every kind of a barnyard bird
Sometimes speaks a pleasant word
   Except our old grey goose.
All she ever has to say
Is a hiss that means, Keep out of my way,
   For humans I have no use!

Sparrows, of course, and robins and wrens
And chickadees, and especially hens
   Are always happily talking.
Only our old grey goose is rude.
When I ask may I hold just one of her brood
   She hisses and goes on walking.

Her babies would like to be friends with me
But she won't ever allow them to be,
   And rudeness is no excuse,
So I turn my back and quack and crow
To my other barnyard friends, to show
   What I think of that old grey goose!

The Grasshopper DAVID McCORD

Down
a
deep
well
a
grasshopper
fell.

By kicking about
He thought to get out.
        He might have known better,
        For that got him wetter.
To kick round and round
Is the way to get drowned,
        And drowning is what
        I should tell you he got.

But
the
well
had
a
rope
that
dangled
some
hope.

And sure as molasses
On one of his passes

He found the rope handy
And up he went, *and he*

it
up
and
it
up
and
it
up
and
it
up
went

And hopped away proper
As any grasshopper.

The Turtle

JACK PRELUTSKY

The turtle's always been inclined
to live within his shell.
But why he cares to be confined,
the turtle does not tell.

The turtle's always satisfied
to slowly creep and crawl,
and never wanders far outside
his living room or hall.

So if you wish to visit him
in his domestic dome,
just knock politely on his shell,
you'll find the turtle home.

A Dog's Tale

AMERICAN FOLK RHYME /
REVISED BY WILLIAM COLE

Little dog sitting by the fireside,
OUT popped a burning coal!
Landed on the doggie's tail
And burned a little hole.
Off ran the little dog,
Looking for a pool
Where he could dip his little tail
To help his tail get cool.
Looking here and looking there,
He began to wail,
When, oh thank goodness, mercy me!
He popped it in a pail!
And wiggle, waggle, wiggle, waggle,
Wiggle, waggle, wiggle, waggle,
Went the doggie's tail.

My Fishes

MARCHETTE CHUTE

My goldfish swim like bits of light,
Silver and red and gold and white.
They flick their tails for joy, and then
They swim around the bowl again.

Cat of Cats

WILLIAM BRIGHTY RANDS

I am the Cat of Cats. I am
   The everlasting cat!
Cunning, and old, and sleek as jam,
   The everlasting cat!
I hunt the vermin in the night —
   The everlasting cat!
For I see best without the light —
   The everlasting cat!

The Mare

HERBERT ASQUITH

Look at the mare of Farmer Giles!
She's brushing her hooves on the mat;

Look at the mare of Farmer Giles!
She's knocked on the door, rat-a-tat!

With a clack of her hoof and a wave of her head
She's tucked herself up in the four-post bed,
And she's wearing the Farmer's hat!

Oliphaunt

J. R. R. TOLKIEN

Grey as a mouse,
Big as a house,
Nose like a snake,
I make the earth shake,
As I tramp through the grass;
Trees crack as I pass.
With horns in my mouth
I walk in the South,
Flapping big ears.
Beyond count of years
I stump round and round,
Never lie on the ground,
Not even to die.
Oliphaunt am I,
Biggest of all,
Huge, old, and tall.
If ever you'd met me,
You wouldn't forget me.
If you never do,
You won't think I'm true;
But old Oliphaunt am I,
And I never lie.

Three Little Guinea Pigs

DANISH NURSERY RHYME /
TRANSLATED BY N. M. BODECKER

Three little guinea pigs
went to see the King.
One brought a rose;
one brought a ring;
one brought a turnip
to give to the King.

Two went back home
neither fatter
nor thinner.
One sat on the Queen's lap
and ate the King's dinner.

Jumpety-Bumpety-Hop

ANONYMOUS

Old Jumpety-Bumpety-Hop-and-Go-One
Was lying asleep on his side in the sun.
This old Kangaroo, he was whisking the flies
(With his long glossy tail) from his ears and his eyes.
Jumpety-Bumpety-Hop-and-Go-One
Was lying asleep on his side in the sun,
Jumpety-Bumpety-Hop!

Furry Bear

A. A. MILNE

If I were a bear
    And a big bear too,
I shouldn't much care
    If it froze or snew;
I shouldn't much mind
    If it snowed or friz —
I'd be all fur-lined
    With a coat like his!

For I'd have fur boots and a brown fur wrap,
And brown fur knickers and a big fur cap.
I'd have a fur muffle-ruff to cover my jaws,
And brown fur mittens on my big brown paws.
With a big brown furry-down up to my head,
I'd sleep all winter in a big fur bed.

22

The Donkey

ANONYMOUS

I saw a donkey
One day old,
His head was too big
For his neck to hold;
His legs were shaky
And long and loose,
They rocked and staggered
And weren't much use.

He tried to gambol
And frisk a bit,
But he wasn't quite sure
Of the trick of it.
His queer little coat
Was soft and grey,
And curled at his neck
In a lovely way.

His face was wistful
And left no doubt
That he felt life needed
Some thinking about.
So he blundered round
In venturesome quest,
And then lay flat
On the ground to rest.

He looked so little
And weak and slim,
I prayed the world
Might be good to him.

Cat

MARY BRITTON MILLER

The black cat yawns,
Opens her jaws,
Stretches her legs,
And shows her claws.

Then she gets up
And stands on four
Long stiff legs
And yawns some more.

She shows her sharp teeth,
She stretches her lip,
Her slice of a tongue
Turns up at the tip.

Lifting herself
On her delicate toes,
She arches her back
As high as it goes.

She lets herself down
With particular care,
And pads away
With her tail in the air.

The Chipmunk's Song

RANDALL JARRELL

In and out the bushes, up the ivy,
Into the hole
By the old oak stump, the chipmunk flashes
Up the pole.

To the feeder full of seeds he dashes,
Stuffs his cheeks,
The chickadee and titmouse scold him.
Down he streaks.

Red as the leaves the wind blows off the maple,
Red as a fox,
Striped like a skunk, the chipmunk whistles
Past the love seat, past the mailbox,

Down the path,
Home to his warm hole stuffed with sweet
Things to eat.
Neat and slight and shining, his front feet

Curled at his breast, he sits there while the sun
Stripes the red west
With its last light: the chipmunk
Dives to his rest.

Kindness to Animals

LAURA E. RICHARDS

Riddle cum diddle cum dido,
My little dog's name is Fido;
   I bought him a wagon,
    And hitched up a dragon,
And off we both went for a ride, oh!

Riddle cum diddle cum doodle,
My little cat's name is Toodle;
   I curled up her hair,
    But she only said, "There!
You have made me look just like a poodle!"

Riddle cum diddle cum dinky,
My little pig's name is Winkie;
   I keep him quite clean
   With the washing machine,
And I rinse him all off in the sinkie.

Choosing Their Names

THOMAS HOOD

Our old cat has kittens three —
What do you think their names should be?

One is tabby with emerald eyes,
   And a tail that's long and slender,
And into a temper she quickly flies
   If you ever by chance offend her.
      I think we shall call her this —
      I think we shall call her that —
Now, don't you think that Pepperpot
      Is a nice name for a cat?

One is black with a frill of white,
   And her feet are all white fur,
If you stroke her she carries her tail upright
   And quickly begins to purr.
      I think we shall call her this —
      I think we shall call her that —
Now, don't you think that Sootikin
      Is a nice name for a cat?

One is a tortoiseshell yellow and black,
　　With plenty of white about him;
If you tease him, at once he sets up his back,
　　He's a quarrelsome one, ne'er doubt him.
　　　　I think we shall call him this —
　　　　I think we shall call him that —
Now, don't you think that Scratchaway
　　　　Is a nice name for a cat?

Our old cat has kittens three
And I fancy these their names will be:
Pepperpot, Sootikin, Scratchaway — there!
Were ever kittens with these to compare?
And we call the old mother —
　　　　Now, what do you think? —
Tabitha Longclaws Tiddley Wink.

The Poor Snail

J. M. WESTRUP

The snail says, "Alas!"
And the snail says, "Alack!
Why must I carry
My house on my back?
You have a home
To go in and out,
Why must mine always be
Carried about?
Not any tables,
Not any chairs,
Not any windows,
Not any stairs,
Pity my misery,
Pity my wail —
For I must always be
Just a poor snail."
But he's terribly slow,
So perhaps it's as well
That his shell is his home,
And his home is his shell.

Frog

CONRAD AIKEN

How nice to be
      a
      speckled
      frog
with all those
      colors
      in
      a
      bog
AND SIT THERE ALL DAY LONG AND SOG
how nice at noon
to keep so cool
just squatting in your private pool
or when enough of THAT you've had
      to sun
      on
      your own lily pad.

But best of all at rise of moon
with you
and all your friends
in tune
as *jug-o'-rum*
and *jing-a-ring*
and trilling *peep-peep-peep*
you sing
till
   listening
         we
            fall
               asleep
                    slowly
              listening
       fall
asleep.

The Tickle Rhyme

IAN SERRAILLIER

"Who's that tickling my back?" said the wall.
"Me," said a small
Caterpillar. "I'm learning
To crawl."

Glowworm

DAVID McCORD

Never talk down to a glowworm —
Such as *What do you knowworm?*
How's it down belowworm?
Guess you're quite a slowworm.
No. Just say
        Helloworm!

Puzzling

WILLIAM COLE

Here's a fact that will cause you to frown —
Instead of growing up, a goose grows down!

The North Wind Doth Blow

ENGLISH NURSERY RHYME

The north wind doth blow,
And we shall have snow,
And what will poor robin do then, poor thing?
He'll sit in a barn,
And keep himself warm,
And hide his head under his wing, poor thing.

Tails

MYRA COHN LIVINGSTON

A dog's tail
    is short
And a cat's tail
    is long,
And a horse has a tail
    that he
    swishes along,
And a fish has a tail
    that can
    help him
    to swim,
And a pig has a tail
    that looks
    curly on him.
All monkeys have tails
And the elephants too.

There are
hundreds of
tails
if
  you
      look
         in
           the
             zoo!

The Caterpillar

EDWARD LUCIE-SMITH

The caterpillar comes to table,
And eats as much as he is able.

"The cabbage-leaf," he mutters, munching,
"Was made for dining, and for lunching."

The gardener shouts: "*My* lunch! *my* dinner!
Be off with you, you ugly sinner!"

But hear the haughty worm reply:
"You'll never be a butterfly."

A Black-nosed Kitten

MARY MAPES DODGE

A black-nosed kitten will slumber all the day;
A white-nosed kitten is ever glad to play;
A yellow-nosed kitten will answer to your call;
And a gray-nosed kitten I wouldn't have at all!

Opossum

WILLIAM JAY SMITH

Have you ever in your life seen a Possum play possum?
Have you ever in your life seen a Possum play dead?
When a Possum is trapped and can't get away
He turns up his toes and lays down his head,
Bats both his eyes and rolls over dead.
But then when you leave him and run off to play,
The Possum that really was just playing possum
Gets up in a flash and scurries away.

The Blame

SHEL SILVERSTEIN

The pie is gone — let's blame it on
the naughty hippopotamus.
And spank him well — if we can tell
exactly where his bottom is.

The Kangaroo

ELIZABETH COATSWORTH

It is a curious thing that you
don't wish to be a kangaroo,
    to hop hop hop
    and never stop
the whole day long and the whole night, too!

To hop across Australian plains
with tails that sweep behind like trains
    and small front paws
    and pointed jaws
and pale neat coats to shed the rains.

If skies be blue, if skies be gray,
they bound in the same graceful way
    into dim space
    at such a pace
that where they go there's none to say!

Familiar Friends

JAMES S. TIPPETT

The horses, the pigs,
And the chickens,
The turkeys, the ducks
And the sheep!
I can see all my friends
From my window
As soon as I waken
From sleep.

The cat on the fence
Is out walking.
The geese have gone down
For a swim.
The pony comes trotting
Right up to the gate;
He knows I have candy
For him.

The cows in the pasture
Are switching
Their tails to keep off
The flies
And the old mother dog
Has come out in the yard
With five pups to give me
A surprise.

Mice and Cat

CLIVE SANSOM

One mouse, two mice,
Three mice, four,
Stealing from their tunnel,
Creeping through the door.

Softly! Softly!
Don't make a sound —
Don't let your little feet
Patter on the ground.

There on the hearthrug,
Sleek and fat,
Soundly sleeping,
Lies old Tom Cat.

If he should hear you,
There'd be no more
Of one mouse, two mice,
Three mice, four.

So please be careful
How far you roam,
For if you should wake him . . .
He'd-chase-you-all-HOME!

Zoo Manners

EILEEN MATHIAS

Be careful what
  You say or do
When you visit the animals
  At the Zoo.

Don't make fun
  Of the Camel's hump —
He's very proud
  Of his noble bump.

Don't laugh too much
  At the Chimpanzee —
He thinks he's as wise
  As you or me.

And the Penguins
  Strutting round the lake
Can understand
  Remarks you make.

Treat them as well
  As they do you,
And you'll always be welcome
  At the Zoo.

The Shark

EDWARD LUCIE-SMITH

The shark has rows
And rows of teeth,
And keeps them safely
Underneath.

He has to swim
Upon his back
When trying to grab you
For a snack.

Brothers

WILLIAM COLE

That handsome little chimpanzee
Looks very much like you — or me!

Birds in the Garden

ANONYMOUS

Greedy little sparrow,
    Great big crow,
Saucy little chickadee,
    All in a row.

Are you very hungry,
    No place to go?
Come and eat my breadcrumbs,
    In the snow.

"Down the stream the swans all glide"

SPIKE MILLIGAN

Down the stream the swans all glide;
It's quite the cheapest way to ride.
Their legs get wet,
Their tummies wetter:
I think after all
The bus is better.

The Lion

SPIKE MILLIGAN

A Lion is fierce:
His teeth can pierce
The skin of a postman's knee.

It serves him right
That, because of his bite,
He gets no letters you see.

Frog

VALERIE WORTH

The spotted frog
Sits quite still
On a wet stone;

He is green
With a luster
Of water on his skin;

His back is mossy
With spots, and green
Like moss on a stone;

His gold-circled eyes
Stare hard
Like bright metal rings;

When he leaps
He is like a stone
Thrown into the pond;

Water rings spread
After him, bright circles
Of green, circles of gold.

Ducks

MARY ANN HOBERMAN

Ducks are lucky,
Don't you think?
When they want to
Take a drink,
All they do is
Duck their bill.
(Doesn't matter
If they spill.)
When they want to
Take a swim,
All they do is
Dive right in;
And they never
Seem to sink.
Ducks are lucky,
Don't you think?

"Here come the elephants, ten feet high..."

JACK PRELUTSKY

Here come the elephants, ten feet high,
elephants, elephants, heads in the sky.
Eleven great elephants intertwined,
one little elephant close behind.

Elephants over and elephants under
elephants bellow with elephant thunder.
Up on pedestals elephants hop,
elephants go and elephants stop.

Elephants quick and elephants slow,
elephants dancing to and fro.
Elephants, elephants twice times six,
elephants doing elephant tricks.

Elephants strutting, elephants strolling,
rollicking elephants frolicking, rolling.
Elephants forming an elephant arch,
elephants marching an elephant march.

Elephants there and elephants here,
elephants cheering an elephant cheer.
Elephants, elephants, trunks unfurled,
in a wonderful, elegant elephant world.

What the Cock and Hen Say

NURSERY RHYME

"Lock the dairy door!
Lock the dairy door!"

"Chickle, chackle, chee!
I haven't got the key!"

Little Miss Tuckett

ENGLISH NURSERY RHYME

Little Miss Tuckett
Sat on a bucket,
Eating some peaches and cream;
There came a grasshopper
And tried to stop her;
But she said, "Go away, or I'll scream."

Three Little Birds

LAURA E. RICHARDS

Three little birds
Sat upon a tree.
The first said "Chirrup!"
The second said "Chee!"
The third said nothing
(The middle one was he),
But sat there a-blinking,
Because he was a-thinking.
"Pee-wit! pee-wit! Yes, that is it!
Pee-wip, pee-wop, pee-wee!"

Three little birds
Sat upon a bough.
The first said, "When is dinner-time?"
The second said "Now!"
The third said nothing
(The middle one was he),
But sat there a-blinking,
Because he was a-thinking,
"Pee-wit! pee-wit! Yes, that is it!
Pee-wip, pee-wop, pee-wee!"

Two little birds flew down to the ground,
And soon, by working very hard,
A fine fat worm they found.
The third flew down between them
(The middle one was he),
And ate it up like winking,
Because he had been thinking.
"Pee-wit! pee-wit! Yes, that is it!
Pee-wip, pee-wop, pee-wee!"

"Quack!" Said the Billy Goat

CHARLES CAUSLEY

"Quack!" said the billy goat,
    "Oink!" said the hen.
"Miaow!" said the little chick
    Running in the pen.

"Hobble-gobble!" said the dog.
    "Cluck!" said the sow.
"Tu-whit tu-whoo!" the donkey said.
    "Baa!" said the cow.

"Hee-haw!" the turkey cried.
    The duck began to moo.
All at once the sheep went,
    "Cock-a-doodle-doo!"

"Bleat! Bleat!" said the owl
    When he began to speak.
"Bow-wow!" said the cock
    Swimming in the creek.

"Cheep-cheep!" said the cat
    As she began to fly.
"Farmer's been and laid an egg —
    That's the reason why."

The Porcupine

KARLA KUSKIN

A porcupine looks somewhat silly.
He also is extremely quilly
And if he shoots a quill at you
Run fast
Or you'll be quilly too.

I would not want a porcupine
To be my loving valentine.

Bears

ELIZABETH COATSWORTH

Bears
have few cares.
When the wind blows cold and the snow drifts deep
they sleep and sleep and sleep and sleep.

Bullfrog Communiqué

MILDRED LUTON

I know a pond where frogs repeat
the water's depth, but not in feet
or yards or inches. Here's the way
they issue a communiqué:
A croaky treble close to shore
repeats his findings o'er and o'er,
ankle deep . . . ankle deep . . . ankle deep
and farther out a baritone
reports from his official zone,
Knee Deep. . . Knee Deep . . . Knee Deep.
And way out in the deepest place
a daddy frog's bull fiddle bass,
BELLY DEEP . . . BELLY DEEP . . . BELLY DEEP.

I waded through that pond one night
and, bless my soul, the frogs are right
ankle deep
             Knee Deep
                          BELLY DEEP!

The Animal Song

ANONYMOUS

Alligator, hedgehog, anteater, bear,
Rattlesnake, buffalo, anaconda, hare.

Bullfrog, woodchuck, wolverine, goose,
Whippoorwill, chipmunk, jackal, moose.

Mud turtle, whale, glowworm, bat,
Salamander, snail, and Maltese cat.

Polecat, dog, wild otter, rat,
Pelican, hog, dodo, and bat.

House rat, toe rat, white deer, doe,
Chickadee, peacock, bobolink, and crow.

Noah's Ark

SHEL SILVERSTEIN

The mice squeak
The cats meow
The cows moo
The dogs bark
The lions roar
The owls hoot
As two by two
By two by two
They walk into
Their wooden zoo
And sit down in the ark

Index of Titles

Index of First Lines

I am the Cat of Cats. I am, 15

I know a pond where frogs repeat, 74

I saw a donkey, 24

If I were a bear, 22

In and out the bushes, up the ivy, 27

It is a curious thing that you, 45

Little dog sitting by the fireside, 14

Little Miss Limberkin, 5

Little Miss Tuckett, 65

"Lock the dairy door!, 63

Look at the mare of Farmer Giles!, 16

My goldfish swim like bits of light, 15

Never talk down to a glowworm —, 36

Old Jumpety-Bumpety-Hop-and-Go-One, 21

Old Noah once he built an ark, 1

One mouse, two mice, 48

Our old cat has kittens —, 30

Pigeon on the roof, 7

"Quack!" said the billy goat, 69

Riddle cum diddle cum dido, 28

That handsome little chimpanzee, 54

The black cat yawns, 26

The caterpillar comes to table, 40

The horses, the pigs, 46

The mice squeak, 76

The north wind doth blow, 37

The pie is gone — let's blame it on, 43

The shark has rows, 52

The snail says, "Alas!," 32

The spotted frog, 58

The turtle's always been inclined, 12

Three little birds, 66

Three little guinea pigs, 20

To whit, 3

Wherever he goes, 6

"Who's that tickling my back?" said the wall, 36

Index of Authors

Acknowledgments

Acknowledgment is made to the following publishers and authors or their representatives for their permission to use copyright material. Every reasonable effort has been made to clear the use of the poems in this volume with the copyright owners. If notified of any omissions the editor and publisher will gladly make the proper corrections in future printings.

Atheneum Publishers, for "Frog," and "Owl," from CATS AND BATS AND THINGS WITH WINGS. Text copyright © 1965 by Conrad Aiken. "Three Little Guinea Pigs," from IT'S RAINING SAID JOHN TWAINING by N. M. Bodecker (A Margaret K. McElderry Book). Copyright © 1973 by N. M. Bodecker.

Elizabeth Coatsworth, for her poem, "Bears."

William Cole, for "The Snail," "Brothers," "Puzzling," "See the animals . . ." Copyright © 1978 by William Cole.

Dennis Dobson Publishers, for two poems by Spike Milligan: "The Lion," from A BOOK OF MILLIGANIMALS, and "Down the stream the swans all glide," from SILLY VERSE FOR KIDS.

E. P. Dutton, for "My Fishes," from RHYMES ABOUT US by Marchette Chute. Copyright © 1974 by Marchette Chute. "Easy Diver," from STREET POEMS by Robert Froman. Copyright © 1971 by Robert Froman. "Furry Bear," from NOW WE ARE SIX by A. A. Milne. Copyright 1927 by E. P. Dutton, renewal © 1955 by A. A. Milne.

Evans Brothers Limited, for "Zoo Manners," by Eileen Mathias and "The Poor Snail," by J. M. Westrup, from COME FOLLOW ME.

Farrar, Straus & Giroux, Inc., for "Frog," from SMALL POEMS by Valerie Worth. Copyright © 1972 by Valerie Worth.

Harcourt Brace Jovanovich, Inc., for "Old Grey Goose," from THE WIZARD IN THE WELL © 1956 by Harry Behn.

Harper & Row Publishers, Inc., for "Familiar Friends," from CRICKETY CRICKET! The Best-Loved Poems of James S. Tippett. Text copyright © 1973 by Martha K. Tippett.

William Heinemann, Ltd., and Macmillan Publishing Co., Inc., for "The Mare," from PILLICOCK HILL by Herbert Asquith.

David Higham Associates Ltd., for "Mice and Cat," from THE GOLDEN UNICORN by Clive Sansom, published by Methuen & Co., Ltd.